Contents

Macmillan Education
4 Crinan Street
London N1 9XW
A division of Springer Nature Limited

Companies and representatives throughout the world

Mimi's Wheel Level 1 Pupil's Book Plus ISBN 978-1-380-01872-4
Mimi's Wheel Level 1 Pupil's Book Plus with Navio App ISBN 978-1-380-02687-3

First published 2019

Original design by Clare Webber
Page make-up by emc design ltd
Illustrated by BluBlu Animation Group Sp. z.o.o. based on original character design by Jose Ignacio Gómez (Nacho Gómez)
Cover design by emc design ltd
Cover illustration by Jose Ignacio Gómez (Nacho Gómez)
Picture research by Lorraine Beck

Author's acknowledgements
I would like to thank everyone at Macmillan Education in the UK, Spain and Mexico who has contributed to the development and production of these materials. I would also like to thank all the teachers who have taken time to read and pilot the materials, and given invaluable feedback at every stage of writing the course. Special thanks as ever go to my husband, Alan, for his encouragement and support, and to our son and daughter, Jamie and Hannah, from whose early childhood days I learnt so much.

The publishers would like to thank Alex Tamulis, São Paulo, Brazil; Ayşegül Sezer, İNO Schools, Turkey; Daniela Araujo Pielli, Alt Idiomas, São Bernardo Do Campo, Brazil; Daniela Pugliese, Milton's College, Buenos Aires, Argentina; Esra Ezici, Turkey; Fernanda Domeniconi Nery Amorim, São Paulo, Brazil; Gabriela Iocolari, English Schoolhouse, Buenos Aires, Argentina; Gulbin Cin, Bahcesehir College, Turkey; Mariana Pastorino, Em Pi Instituto de Inglés, Santa Fe, Argentina; Mariné Ortiz, Warrington, Buenos Aires, Argentina; Paola Daniela Tuninetti, Academia Argüello, Córdoba, Argentina; Silvana Paola Accardo, Escuela Cooperativa Mundo Nuevo Instituto Casa de Jesús, Buenos Aires, Argentina.

The authors and publishers would like to thank the following for permission to reproduce their photographs:
Alamy Stock Photo/Arcaid Images p81(garden), Alamy Stock Photo/Andrey Armyagov p97(coat), Alamy Stock Photo/Michael Burrell pp15, 95(eraser), pp76, 101(bucket), Alamy Stock Photo/Robert Hicks pp15, 95(pencil), Alamy Stock Photo/Wilawan Khasawong p95(table), Alamy Stock Photo/Martin Lee pp55, 59, 61, 99(sandwich), Alamy Stock Photo/MBI p9(sister), Alamy Stock Photo/Pick and Mix Images pp76, 101(spade), Alamy Stock Photo/StockPhotosArt - Sweets pp55, 61, 99(cookie), Alamy Stock Photo/Steve Taylor ARPS p81(crab), Alamy Stock Photo/Andrew Twort pp35, 97(hat), Alamy Stock Photo/SABAR UDIN pp75, 76, 101(sea), Alamy Stock Photo/Wavebreak Media ltd pp5, 6(c,grandmother,grandfather), 94, Alamy Stock Photo/Björn Wylezich pp15, 95(book); **Getty Images**/AlexStar pp24, 64(modelling clay), Getty Images/artisteer pp65, 100(mouse), Getty Images/aurigadesign p71(bl), Getty Images/bazilfoto pp65, 100(bird), 69(r), Getty Images/Corvalol pp55, 61, 99(apple), Getty Images/cynoclub p69(mr), Getty Images/Davies and Starr pp75, 76, 101(crab), Getty Images/Dorling Kindersley pp35, 97(tshirt), Getty Images/Eliza317 pp59, 61, 99(water), Getty Images/EyeEm/Cristina Catlin pp25, 96(eye), Getty Images/EyeEm/Massimiliano Clari pp66, 100(cat), Getty Images/EyeEm/Frank Mcclintock p71(tl), Getty Images/EyeEm/Iain Mcconnell p81(cat), Getty Images/Aaron Foster p81(sea), Getty Images/Marvin Fox p96(teeth), Getty Images/GlobalP pp65, 100(rabbit), Getty Images/Alexandra Grablewski p9(brother), Getty Images/harmpeti p55, 59, 61, 99(banana), Getty Images/heinteh pp35, 97(shorts), Getty Images/Image Source p51(br), Getty Images/iStockphoto pp25, 96(mouth), Getty Images/Ivan-balvan pp35, 97(shoes), Getty Images/jskiba pp75, 76, 101(shell), Getty Images/kbwills pp59, 61, 99(juice), Getty Images/kickers pp25, 96(nose), Getty Images/Dave King pp65, 100(fish), Getty Images/lucielang pp14, 24, 34, 44, 54, 64, 74, 84(crayons), pp15, 95(crayon), Getty Images/A. Martin UW Photography p81(fish), Getty Images/Microzoa p81(sea), Getty Images/mrs p96(hair), Getty Images/parinyabinsuk p14(pegs), Getty Images/Jose Luis Pelaez Inc pp9, 94(grandfather, grandmother), Getty Images/photovideostock pp75, 76, 101(sand), Getty Images/pzAxe p97(boots), Getty Images/Ridofranz p9(father), Getty Images/Kinzie Riehm p51(tr), Getty Images/Techin24 pp25, 96(ear); **iStockphoto**/alex_kz pp 34, 44, 74, 84(glue); **PHOTODISC** pp66, 100(dog); **Shutterstock**/brillenstimmer p95(chair), Shutterstock/Johannes Kornelius p69(fish); **Spectrecom** pp9(tr, mother), 12(tr), 19, 22(tr), 29(c,tr), 32(tr), 39, 42(tr), 49(t), 52(tr),59(tr), 62(tr), 69, 72(tr), 79, 82(tr); **www.imagesource.com** pp14, 54(string).

Commissioned photography by Helen Marsden pp6(tr), 7(tl), 11, 14(1,2,3), 16, 17(tl), 21, 22(tl), 24(1,2,3), 26, 27(tl), 31(ear, eye, boy, girl), 32 (Sophie,Tom), 34(wool, 1,2,3), 36, 37(tl), 41, 42(bl,bm,br), 44(tissue paper, 1,2,3), 45, 46, 47(tl), 49(scooter, teddy), 51(tl, bl), 54(stickers, coathanger, 1,2,3), 56, 57(tl), 59(Sophie,Tom), 61(tr), 64(1,2,3), 66(c), 67(tl), 71(tr), 74(1,2,3), 76(c), 77(tl), 81(tr), 84(1,2,3), 98.

These materials may contain links for third party websites. We have no control over, and are not responsible for, the contents of such third party websites. Please use care when accessing them.

The inclusion of any specific companies, commercial products, trade names or otherwise does not constitute or imply its endorsement or recommendation by Springer Nature Limited.

Printed and bound in Spain

2023 2022 2021 2020 2019
10 9 8 7 6 5 4 3 2 1

Hello
Welcome!

Listen, point and sing *Hello, hello, hello.* Stick the stickers of Mimi and Dylan.
Language: Mimi, Dylan; boy, girl; Hello, I'm (Mimi).

1:13

3

Hello

Listen, point and sing *Welcome to the Big Wheel!* Colour the pod red. Say.
Language: Mummy, Daddy, Mimi, Dylan; Big Wheel; red

1:14   hello

4

Family
The Big Wheel

1:16 1:17 hello

Listen, point and repeat. Listen and play. Stick the family stickers. Say.
Language: mummy, daddy, brother, sister; blue, green, red, yellow

5

Family

**Listen and find the new family members. Listen, point and sing *Where's your grandma?*
Colour the circle next to Grandpa red. Colour the circle next to Grandma blue. Ask and say.**
Language: mummy, daddy, grandma, grandpa, brother, sister; Where's your (grandma)? Here.

6

Story

1:21

hello

Watch. Listen to the story *The Big Wheel*. Colour the character on the wheel with Zara Zebra. Stick the story sticker. Ask and say. Language: mummy, daddy, grandma, grandpa, brother, sister; Big Wheel; blue, orange, pink, yellow; Where's (Grandma)? Here.

Family

Watch. Listen, point and sing *The Big Wheel song*. Colour Mimi. Say.
Language: mummy, grandma, sister; Big Wheel; Here we go. Round and round.

8

Life skills

 Family

  1:24   hello

Watch. Listen and point. Follow and draw a path to connect the pictures in order. Trace around Mummy. Ask and say. Language: mummy, daddy, grandma, grandpa, brother, sister; Where's your (sister)? Here. This is my (mummy).

Lesson 6

Values   I love my family

Family

1:25

Listen, point and sing *I love my family*. **Colour the frame red. Say.**

Language: mummy, daddy, grandma, grandpa, brother, sister; I love my (mummy).

SOCIAL AND
EMOTIONAL
LEARNING

10

1:26

hello

Listen and point. Colour the wheels. Say.
Language: round, wheel; This is a (wheel). Wheels go round and round.

Watch. Listen, point and sing *The wheels on the bus*. **Colour the circles under the family members in the song. Say.** Language: mummy, daddy, brother, sister; bus, wheels; The wheels on the bus go round and round.

12

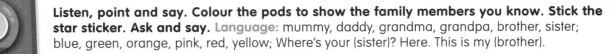

Listen, point and say. Colour the pods to show the family members you know. Stick the star sticker. Ask and say. Language: mummy, daddy, grandma, grandpa, brother, sister; blue, green, orange, pink, red, yellow; Where's your (sister)? Here. This is my (brother).

Project

COOPERATIVE LEARNING

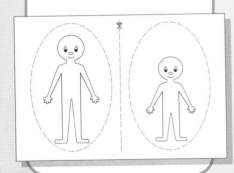

1

2

3

Our families

Choose and colour a member of your family. Make a family display. Ask and say.
Language: mummy, daddy, grandma, grandpa, brother, sister; Where's your (grandpa)? Here.
This is my (sister). I love my (daddy).

14

Classroom
Mimi's first day at school

Listen, point and repeat. Listen and play. Stick the classroom object stickers. Say.

Language: book, crayon, pencil, rubber; blue, orange, pink, yellow

Lesson 2 Language

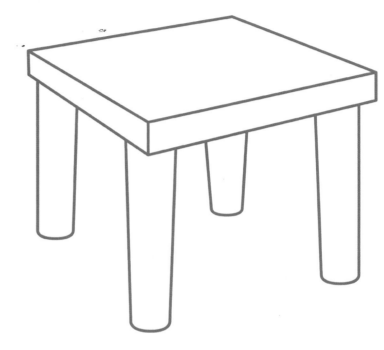

Listen and find the new classroom objects. Listen, point and sing *Stand up! Sit down!* Colour the chair red and the table blue. Point and say. Language: book, chair, crayon, pencil, rubber, table; Sit down. Stand up. Look! It's a (chair).

Watch. Listen to the story *Mimi's first day at school*. Colour the characters who find the classroom objects. Stick the story sticker. Ask and say. Language: book, crayon, pencil, rubber; happy, sad; Look! It's a (crayon). Where's your (book)? Here. / I don't know. I'm (sad).

17

Watch. Listen, point and sing *Where's your book?* Follow and draw the path through the maze. Ask and say. Language: book, crayon, pencil, rubber; happy, sad; Where's your (book)? Here. / I don't know. I'm (happy).

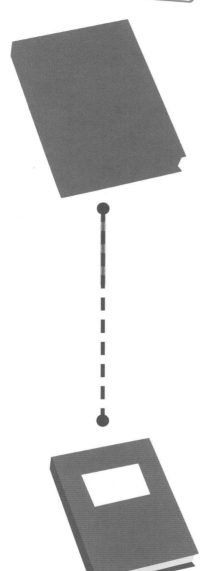

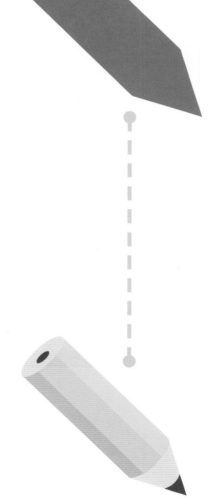

Watch. Listen and point. Trace to match the classroom objects. Ask and say.
Language: book, pencil; blue, yellow; Where's your (book)? Here. What colour is your (book)? It's (blue).

Values I'm your friend

Listen, point and sing *I'm your friend*. **Draw and colour a picture of a friend. Say.** Language: care, friend, happy, sad; I care. I'm your friend.

SOCIAL AND
EMOTIONAL
LEARNING

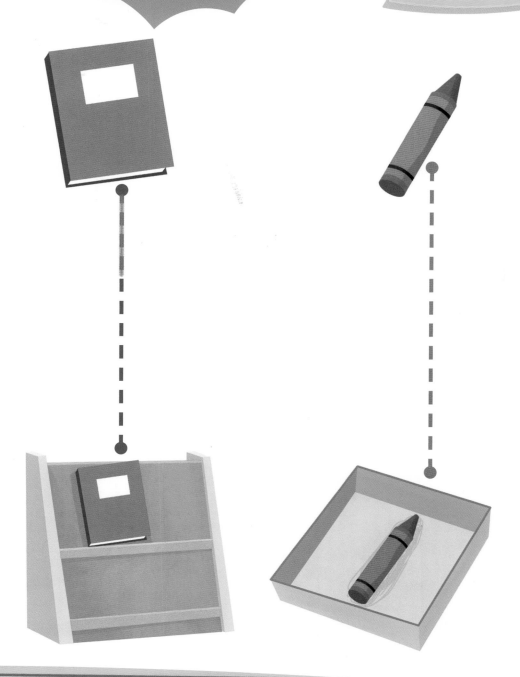

Listen and point. Trace to match the book and crayon to where they belong. Say.
Language: book, crayon; shelf, tray; I put the (crayon) (in) the (tray).

1:39

Classroom

Watch. Listen, point and sing *This is the way I say hello*. **Follow and draw the path from Sophie and Tom to the school. Say.** Language: bye bye, hello; friends, school; This is the way I say (hello).

Listen, point and say. Colour the words you know. Stick the star sticker. Ask and say. Language: book, chair, crayon, pencil, rubber, table; colours; It's a (crayon). Where's your (book)? Here. What colour is your (book)? It's (blue).

Project

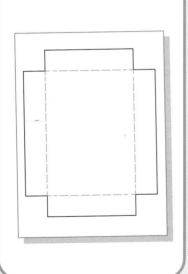

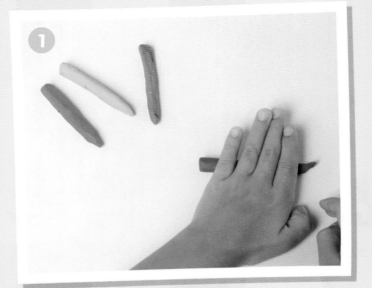

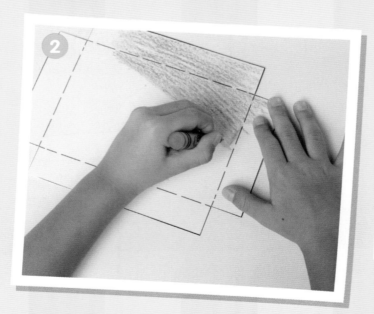

Our crayons

Make some crayons and colour a tray. Put your crayons together in the trays.
Ask and say. Language: crayon, tray; colours; It's a (crayon). It's (red). Where's the (blue) crayon?
Here. What colour is your (crayon)? It's (green). I put the crayon in the tray.

24

My face
Splash!

Listen, point and repeat. Listen and play. Stick the face stickers. Say.
Language: ear, eye, mouth, nose; blue, green, pink, red

2:01   hello   2:02

Listen and find the new parts of the face. Listen, point and sing *I've got two eyes*. Trace to match Sophie's hair and Tom's teeth. Say. Language: ears, eyes, hair, mouth, nose, teeth; I've got (a nose). I've got (two) (eyes).

  2:06   hello

Watch. Listen to the story *Splash!* Colour the boat from the story. Stick the story sticker.
Say. Language: ears, eyes, mouth, nose; boy, girl; water; I've got (two) (eyes). It's (a boy) in the water.

My face

Watch. Listen, point and sing *Two eyes, two ears.* **Follow and draw paths to match the pictures of Mimi and Dylan. Colour the splashes in the water. Point and say.**
Language: ears, eyes, mouth, nose; boy, girl; It's (a boy) in the water.

28

  2:09  hello

Watch. Listen and point. Colour the puppet's eyes and nose. Say.
Language: ears, eyes, hair, mouth, nose; colours; I've got (a red) (mouth).

Lesson 6

Values I'm happy I'm me

My face

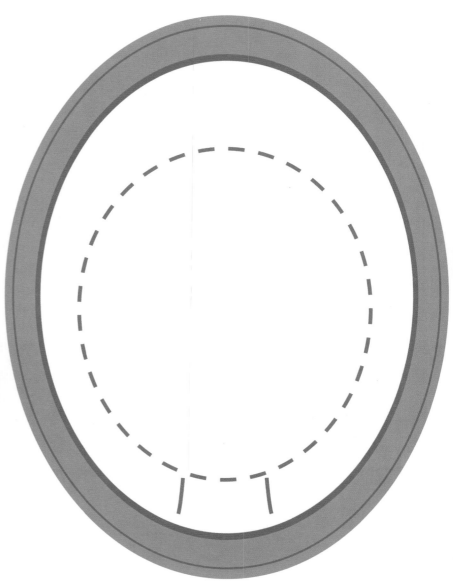

Listen, point and sing *I'm happy I'm me*. **Trace and draw a picture of your face. Say. Language:** ears, eyes, hair, mouth, nose, teeth; happy, special; My (eyes) are special.

SOCIAL AND EMOTIONAL LEARNING

30

My face

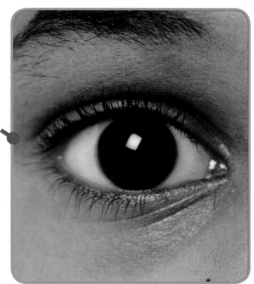

Listen and point. Trace to match the pictures. Say.

Language: hear, see; ears, eyes; I (see) with my (eyes).

My face

Watch. Listen, point and sing *Here are my ears*. Follow and draw a path to connect the pictures in order. Say. Language: ears, eyes, hands, mouth, nose, teeth, toes; Here is my (nose). Here are my (eyes).

Listen, point and say. Colour the words you know. Stick the star sticker. Say.
Language: ears, eyes, hair, mouth, nose, teeth; I've got (hair).

Project

COOPERATIVE LEARNING

1

2

3

Our faces

Colour and decorate a face. Make a faces display. Ask and say. Language: ears, eyes, hair, mouth, nose, teeth; boy, girl; colours; It's (a girl). I've got (red) (hair). I've got (green) (eyes). Where's (Maria)? Here. What colour is your (nose)? It's (pink).

Clothes
Time to get dressed!

Listen, point and repeat. Listen and play. Stick the clothes stickers. Say.
Language: hat, shoes, shorts, T-shirt; orange, pink, red, yellow

2:14 hello 2:15

 2:16   2:17   hello

Listen and find the new clothes. Listen, point and sing _The clothes song_. Follow and draw paths to match the photos. Say. Language: boots, coat, hat, shoes, shorts, T-shirt; Put on your (hat).

Clothes

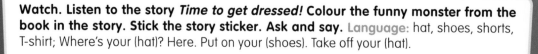

Watch. Listen to the story *Time to get dressed!* **Colour the funny monster from the book in the story. Stick the story sticker. Ask and say.** Language: hat, shoes, shorts, T-shirt; Where's your (hat)? Here. Put on your (shoes). Take off your (hat).

Clothes

Watch. Listen, point and sing *Where's your T-shirt?* Colour the circle to show the correct way to put on the clothes. Ask and say.

Language: hat, shoes, shorts, T-shirt; Where are your (shorts)? Here. Put on your (shoes).

Lesson 5 Speaking

Life skills

Watch. Listen and point. Trace to match Auntie Jenny's hat, Sophie's coat and Tom's boots. Ask and say. Language: boots, coat, hat; Where's your (coat)? Where are your (boots)? Here. Put on your (hat).

Listen, point and sing *I'm tidy*. Colour the star on the picture which shows the clothes in the correct place. Say. Language: boots, coat, hat, shoes; tidy; I'm tidy. I put my (coat) away.

SOCIAL AND EMOTIONAL LEARNING

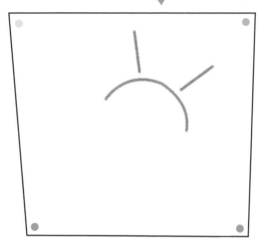

2:24

Listen and point. Draw the sunny and rainy weather in the correct place. Say.
Language: boots, coat, hat, shoes, shorts, T-shirt; rainy, sunny; It's (rainy). I put on my (coat).

Watch. Listen, point and sing *Incy, wincy spider*. Trace to match the pictures to the actions. Say.
Language: spider; rain, sunshine

The funny monster

Listen, point and say. Colour the words you know. Stick the star sticker. Ask and say.
Language: boots, coat, hat, shoes, shorts, T-shirt; Put on your (hat). Take off your (coat).
Where's your (T-shirt)? Where are your (shorts)? Here.

hello

2:26

Project

COOPERATIVE LEARNING

1

2

3

Our clothes

Choose and colour a picture of clothes for sunny or rainy weather. Make a weather display. Ask and say.
Language: boots, coat, hat, shoes, shorts, T-shirt; rainy, sunny; colours; It's (rainy). I put on my (coat). Where's your (hat)?
Where are your (shorts)? Here. What colour is your (coat)? It's (blue). What colour are your (shorts)? They're (red).

Toys
The old toy box

Listen, point and repeat. Listen and play. Stick the toy stickers. Say.
Language: ball, car, doll, teddy; blue, green, orange, yellow

2:27 hello 2:28

Listen and find the new toys. Listen, point and sing *What's this?* Trace to match the scooter and the train. Ask and say.
Language: ball, car, doll, scooter, teddy, train; What's this? It's a (train).

46

Toys

Watch. Listen to the story *The old toy box*. Colour the teddy from the story. Stick the story sticker. Ask and say.

Language: ball, teddy, train; What's this? It's a (train). Let's play with the (ball).

Watch. Listen, point and sing *Let's look in the toy box.*
Find and colour the toys. Say.
Language: ball, teddy, train; Let's play with the (ball).

Speaking

Life skills

Watch. Listen and point. Trace to circle Tom's favourite toy red and Sophie's favourite toy green. Draw a picture of your favourite toy. Ask and say. Language: ball, car, doll, scooter, teddy, train; What's this? It's my (ball). What's your favourite toy? It's my (teddy).

Values We play together

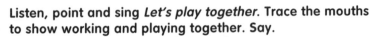

Listen, point and sing *Let's play together*. Trace the mouths to show working and playing together. Say.
Language: play, work; Let's (play) together.

SOCIAL AND EMOTIONAL LEARNING

50

Listen and point. Follow and draw paths to match the activities to the places. Say.
Language: classroom, playground; play, work; I (play) in the (playground).

Watch. Listen, point and say *Bouncy ball*. **Trace the line of the bouncy ball. Say.**
Language: ball; big, bouncy, round; numbers 1–3

2:38

hello

**Listen, point and say. Colour the words you know. Stick the star sticker.
Ask and say.** Language: ball, car, doll, scooter, teddy, train; What's this?
It's a (train). Let's play with the (car). What's your favourite toy? It's my (doll).

2:39   hello

Project

COOPERATIVE LEARNING

1

2

3

Our toys

Colour and decorate a toy. Make a toy mobile. Ask and say.
Language: ball, doll, teddy, train; colours; What's this? It's a (teddy). Let's play with the (ball).
Where's the (red) (train)? Here. What's your favourite toy? It's the (teddy).

54

Food
The picnic

Listen, point and repeat. Listen and play. Stick the food stickers. Say.
Language: apple, banana, biscuit, sandwich; blue, green, pink, red

3:01   hello   3:02

 3:03   3:04   hello

Listen and find the new food words. Listen, point and sing *I like bananas*. Colour the faces and trace to match them to the water and the juice. Point and say.
Language: apples, bananas, biscuits, juice, sandwiches, water; I like (bananas).

  3:06   hello

Watch. Listen to the story *The picnic*. Trace to circle the picnic lunch in the story. Stick the story sticker. Ask and say. Language: banana, biscuit, juice, sandwich; I'm hungry. Can I have my lunch, please? Here's a (sandwich) for you. Thank you. I like (bananas).

Food

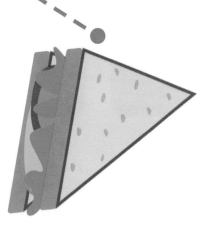

Watch. Listen, point and sing *I'm hungry*. **Trace to match the characters to the food they give Mimi. Point and say.** Language: banana, biscuit, sandwich; I'm hungry. Here's a (sandwich) for you. Thank you.

  3:09   hello

Watch. Listen and point. Trace to circle what Sophie asks for in red and what Tom asks for in blue. Ask and say. Language: banana, juice, sandwich, water; Are you hungry? Can I have (a sandwich), please? Here you are. Thank you. I like (bananas).

Listen, point and sing *Two little words*. **Colour the pictures of Mimi saying 'please' and 'thank you'. Say.**
Language: please, thank you

Food

3:11 | hello

Listen and point. Colour the circles green to show what we eat and blue to show what we drink. Say. Language: drink, eat; apples, bananas, biscuits, juice, sandwiches, water; I eat (apples). I drink (water).

Food

Watch. Listen, point and sing *Ten little apples.* **Colour and count the apples and oranges. Say.** Language: apple, orange; little; tree; numbers 1–10

Listen, point and say. Colour the words you know. Stick the star sticker. Ask and say.
Language: apple, banana, biscuit, juice, sandwich, water; I'm hungry. Can I have (a biscuit), please?
Here you are. Here's (a banana) for you. Thank you. I like (sandwiches).

COOPERATIVE LEARNING

1

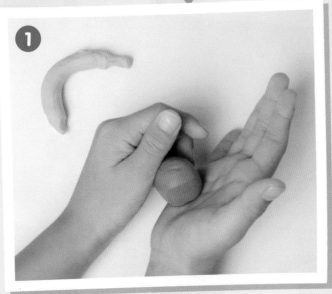

2

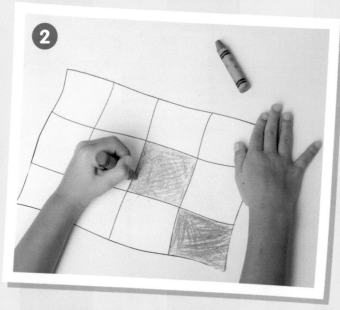

3

Our picnics

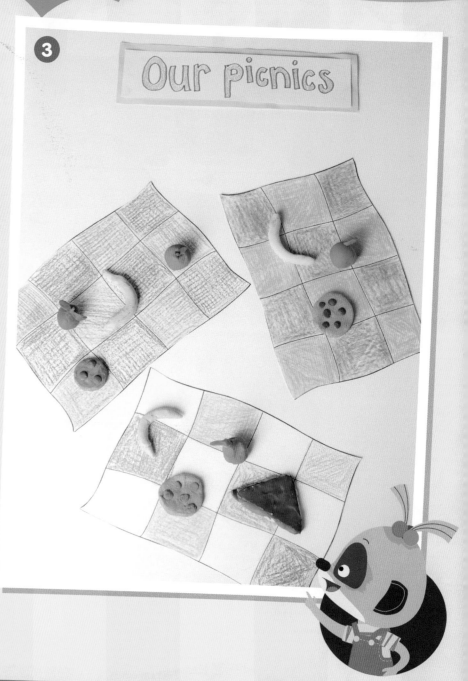

Make food you like for a picnic and colour a picnic blanket. Make a picnic display. Ask and say.

Language: apple, banana, biscuit, juice, sandwich, water; I'm hungry. Are you hungry? Can I have (a biscuit), please? Here you are. Here's (a biscuit) for you. Thank you. I like (sandwiches). What colour is the (apple)? It's (green).

Pets
The little dog

Listen, point and repeat. Listen and play. Stick the pet stickers. Say.
Language: bird, fish, mouse, rabbit; orange, pink, red, yellow

3:14 hello 3:15

Listen and find the new pets. Listen, point and sing *I've got a cat.* **Trace to match the cat and the dog. Say. Language:** bird, cat, dog, fish, mouse, rabbit; I've got a (mouse).

Watch. Listen to the story *The little dog*. Trace to circle the animal in the story. Stick the story sticker. Ask and say. Language: cat, dog, rabbit; mummy; happy, sad; Is this your mummy? Yes, it is. / No, it isn't. It's a (rabbit). I'm (happy).

Story Song

Watch. Listen, point and sing *I'm a little dog*. **Colour the little dog's mummy. Ask and say.**

Language: cat, dog, rabbit; mummy; happy, sad; Is this your mummy? Yes, it is. / No, it isn't.
It's a (rabbit). I'm (happy).

Life skills

Watch. Listen and point. Colour the circles to show the colours of Sophie and Tom's pets. Ask and say. Language: bird, fish; blue, orange; I've got a (bird). Is this your (fish)? Yes, it is. / No, it isn't. This is my (fish). My fish is (orange).

Values I'm kind to you

Listen, point and sing *I'm kind to you.*
Colour the faces to show how you're kind. Say.
Language: I'm kind to you. I help you.

SOCIAL AND
EMOTIONAL
LEARNING

Lesson 7 · Content

Pets

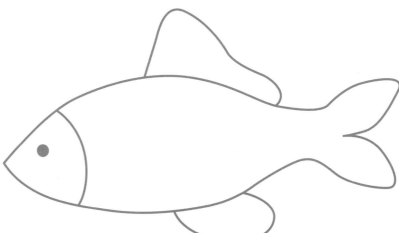

Listen and point. Colour the animal that flies red. Colour the animal that swims green. Say.
Language: fly, swim; birds, fish; Birds fly. Fish swim.

3:24

hello

71

Pets

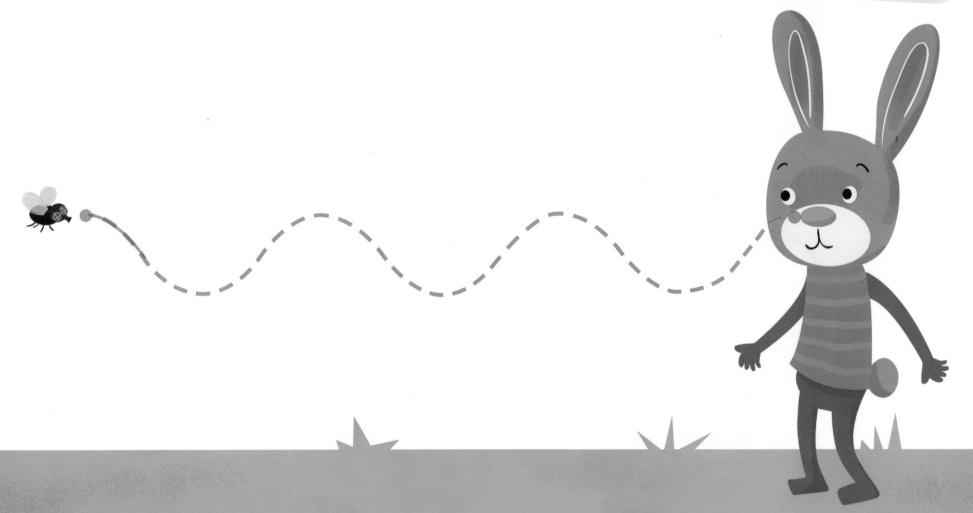

Watch. Listen, point and sing *Little Peter Rabbit.* **Trace the line of the fly to Peter Rabbit's nose. Say.**

Language: fly, rabbit; nose; little; Little Peter Rabbit's got a fly on his nose.

Listen, point and say. Colour the words you know. Stick the star sticker.
Ask and say. Language: bird, cat, dog, fish, mouse, rabbit; I've got a (mouse).
Is this your (cat)? Yes, it is. / No, it isn't. This is my (mouse).

COOPERATIVE LEARNING

1

2

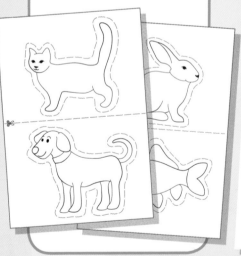

3

Our pets

hello

Choose and colour your favourite pet. Make a poster of your favourite pets. Ask and say.
Language: cat, dog, fish, rabbit; colours; Is this your (cat)? Yes, it is. / No, it isn't. I've got a (dog). What's this?
It's a (cat). Where's the (yellow) (rabbit)? Here. This is my (fish). What colour is your (fish)? It's (orange).

Listen, point and repeat. Listen and play. Stick the seaside stickers. Say.
Language: crab, sand, sea, shell; blue, green, orange, yellow

hello

3:27 3:28

75

Listen and find the new seaside words. Listen, point and sing
I can see the sea. **Match the photos to the picture. Say.**

Language: bucket, crab, sand, sea, shell, spade; I can see a (crab). Me too.

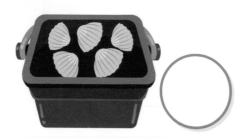

Watch. Listen to the story *Five little crabs*. Colour the circle next to the bucket in the story. Stick the story sticker. Ask and say. Language: bucket, crab, sand, sea, spade; numbers 1–5; little; I can see (five) little crabs. Me too. How many little crabs? (Five).

Watch. Listen, point and sing *One, two, three, four, five little crabs.*
Colour and count the crabs. Ask and say.
Language: bucket, crab, sea; little; numbers 1–5; How many little crabs? (Five).

Watch. Listen and point. Trace to circle the number of shells in Tom and Sophie's buckets. Ask and say. Language: bucket, sand, sea, shell; pink; numbers 1–5; I can see (shells). How many (shells)? (Four). What colour are the (shells)? They're (pink).

Listen, point and sing *I love our world*. Colour the sea blue and the trees green. Say.

Language: sea, trees; blue, green; I love the (blue) (sea).

SOCIAL AND EMOTIONAL LEARNING

Seaside

3:37

hello

Listen and point. Match the animals to where they live. Say.
Language: land, water; cat, crab, fish; (Fish) live in (water). (Cats) live on (land).

Seaside

Watch. Listen, point and sing *One, two, three, four, five.* **Trace to circle the animals in the song. Point and say.**
Language: crab, fish, shell; numbers 1–10

Listen, point and say. Colour the words you know. Stick the star sticker. Ask and say.
Language: bucket, crab, sand, sea, shell, spade; numbers 1–3; colours; I can see (a bucket). Me too.
How many (shells)? (Three). What colour are the (shells)? They're (pink).

Project

COOPERATIVE LEARNING

1

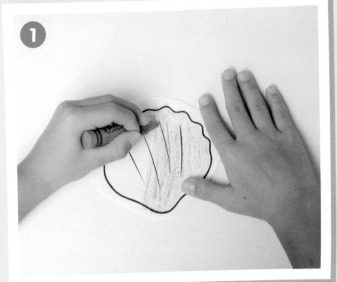

2

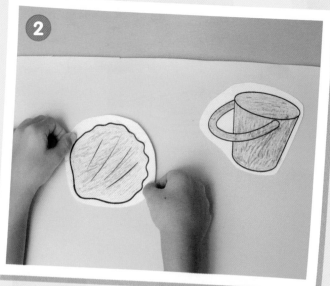

3

The seaside

Colour and decorate an object from the seaside. Make a seaside display. Ask and say. Language: bucket, crab, sand, sea, shell, spade; colours; numbers; I can see (a shell). Me too! How many (crabs)? (Five). Is this your (bucket)? Yes, it is. / No, it isn't. I've got (a spade). What's this? It's (a crab). Where's the (green) (bucket)? Here.

Colours

Listen, point and say. Colour the balls so they are the same.
Language: blue, red, yellow

Listen, point and say. Colour the butterfly so the wings are the same.
Language: green, orange, pink

1 2 3

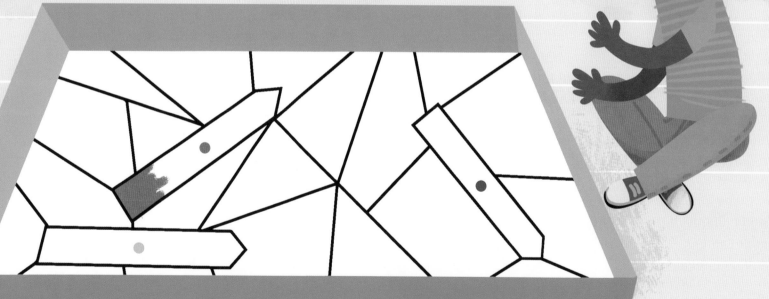

Listen, point and say. Colour and count the crayons.
Language: one, two, three

Numbers 1 2 3 4 5

1

2

3

4

5

Listen, point and say. Colour the eyes of the monsters. Count and say.
Language: one, two, three, four, five

Shapes

Listen, point and say. Trace the circles.
Language: circle

Shapes

Listen, point and say. Trace and colour the squares.
Language: square

3:45 · hello

Concepts

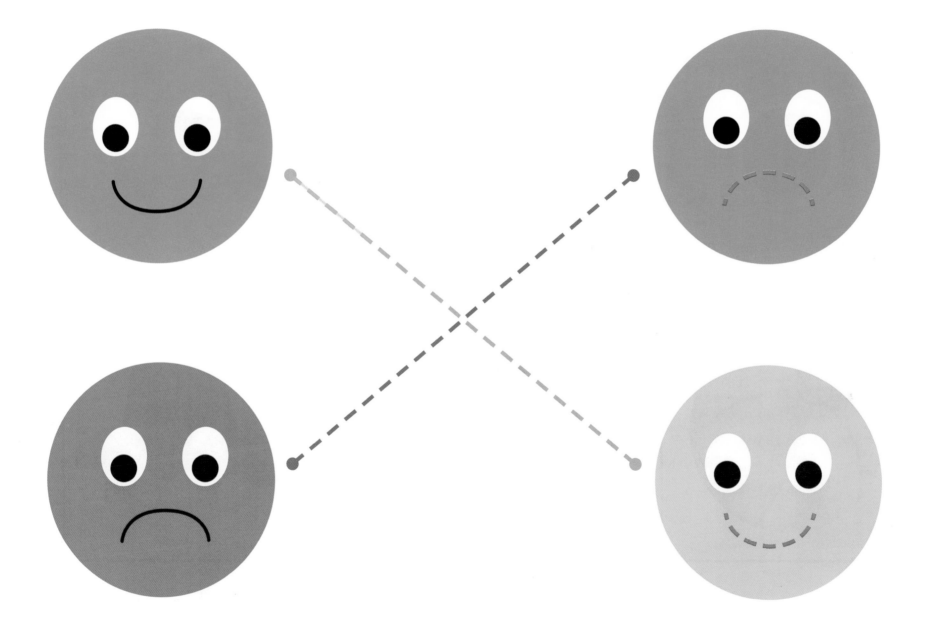

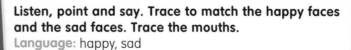

Listen, point and say. Trace to match the happy faces and the sad faces. Trace the mouths.

Language: happy, sad

Concepts

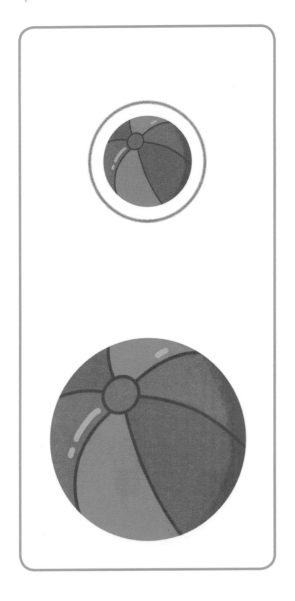

Listen, point and say. Circle the small things.
Language: big, small

Listen, point and say. Trace the lines to show up and down.
Language: up, down

Picture Dictionary

Language: mummy, daddy, grandma, grandpa, brother, sister

Classroom

Language: book, chair, crayon, pencil, rubber, table

Picture Dictionary

My face

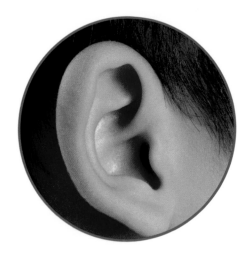

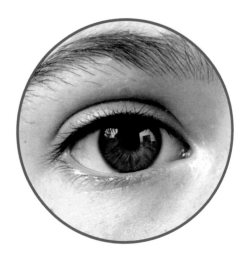

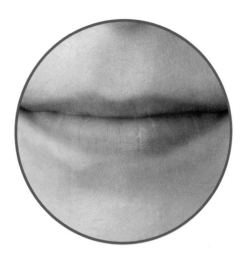

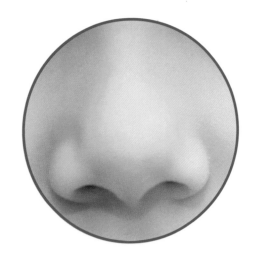

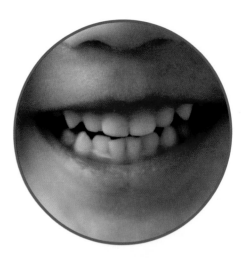

Language: ear, eye, hair, mouth, nose, teeth

Picture Dictionary

Language: boots, coat, hat, shoes, shorts, T-shirt

Picture Dictionary

Language: ball, car, doll, scooter, teddy, train

Picture Dictionary

Language: apple, banana, biscuit, juice, sandwich, water

Picture Dictionary

Language: bird, cat, dog, fish, mouse, rabbit

Picture Dictionary

Language: bucket, crab, sand, sea, shell, spade

Festivals

Carnival

3:49 hello 3:50

Listen, point and say. Listen and sing *Carnival parade.* **Colour and count the Carnival masks. Language:** Carnival, mask, parade; dance, sing; numbers 1–5

Festivals

International Family Day

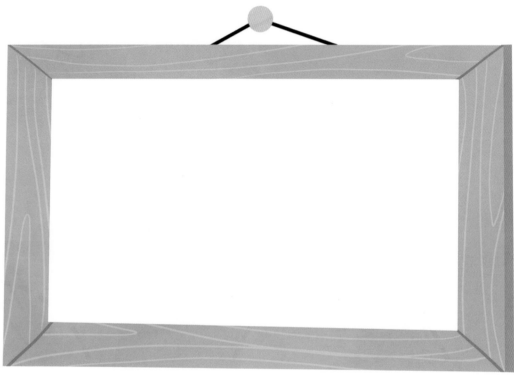

Listen, point and say. Listen and sing *Happy Family Day*. Draw a picture of your family. Language: happy, family; mummy, daddy, grandma, grandpa, brother, sister

3:53 hello 3:54

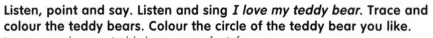

Listen, point and say. Listen and sing *I love my teddy bear.* **Trace and colour the teddy bears. Colour the circle of the teddy bear you like.**

Language: brown; teddy bear; eyes, feet, fur